IMAGES
of America

CLARKSVILLE AND
RED RIVER COUNTY

ON THE COVER: Arriving by carriage from the Texas and Pacific Depot in 1892, Gov. Jim Hogg visited Clarksville. William Gordon is driving the open landau carriage, and Governor Hogg is in the rear seat with his prominent white hat. In front of the Transcontinental Saloon are the Red River Rifles with Morgan Graves, the commander, standing just under the flag. The trees in the background conceal the old Donoho Hotel. In the distance rises the courthouse tower. (Courtesy of Red River County Historical Society Collection, gift of Mildred Gordon Spencer.)

IMAGES
of America

CLARKSVILLE AND RED RIVER COUNTY

Red River County Historical Society

ARCADIA
PUBLISHING

Published by Arcadia Publishing
Charleston SC, Chicago IL, Portsmouth NH, San Francisco CA

Library of Congress Control Number: 2010921999

For all general information contact Arcadia Publishing at:
Telephone 843-853-2070
Fax 843-853-0044
E-mail sales@arcadiapublishing.com
For customer service and orders:
Toll-Free 1-888-313-2665

Visit us on the Internet at www.arcadiapublishing.com

CONTENTS

ACKNOWLEDGMENTS

The majority of the photographs in this book are from the collection of the Red River County Historical Society. Many of the photographs were collected and documented for the historical society by the late Georgia Swann VanDyke Fowler. Without her long years of work and dedication to the project, the collection would not have been possible. For this, we are forever indebted to her. The following individuals, families, and organizations also contributed photographs used in this book: the Eugene W. Bowers collection, Anne Russell Evetts, Mary Humphrey Hausler, Sam Lennox Hocker, Amy Marable McBride, John M. Nichols, Jan Jones Smith, Richard D. "Dick" Wren, First Presbyterian Church, St. John Lutheran Church, St. Joseph Catholic Church, the Pat C. and Lela May Wooley Beadle family, the Elmer Bentsen family, and the Jim Clark family.

The most utilized sources of information for this book were Pat B. Clark's *Clarksville and Old Red River County*, Eugene W. Bower's *Red River Dust*, The Red River County Historical Society's *Red River Recollections*, the archives of the Red River County Historical Society, and The Texas Historical Commission's *Handbook of Texas*.

This book is dedicated to the memory of Martha, David, and Bagby Lennox of the Lennox Foundation, which has provided countless funds to aid in the preservation and beautification of Clarksville and Red River County. Without their generosity, many of our preservation projects would not have been possible.

—Jim Clark
Red River County Historical Society

To learn more about the history of Clarksville and Red River County, contact:

Red River County Historical Society
P. O. Box 1261
Clarksville, Texas 75426

For Red River County tourist information, contact:

Historic Red River County Chamber of Commerce
101 North Locust Street
Clarksville, Texas 75426
903-427-2645

INTRODUCTION

Clarksville and Red River County have a very proud history. Archeological evidence indicates that Native Americans occupied parts of Red River County lands as early as 1500 B.C. At the time of the first European contact, Caddo Indians, an agricultural people with a highly developed culture, occupied this area. During the 1820s, bands of Shawnee, Delaware, and Kickapoo Indians immigrated into what is now Red River County, settling along the banks of the creeks that still bear their names. Some of the earliest Anglo settlements were along the Red River, which included Pecan Point, Burkham Settlement, and Jonesboro. Claiborne Wright first settled at Pecan Point around 1816. Court was first held in this district at Jonesboro, which was then considered to be a part of Miller County, Arkansas. Court was later held at LaGrange, which was located near the present-day community of Madras.

In 1833, James and Isabella Clark left the mosquito-infested community of Jonesboro for the prairie and settled near a spring in a small skirt of timber, which was to become present day Clarksville. The area was still in dispute over who was to govern it. Although many of the early settlers seem to have regarded the area as a part of the United States, when the United States government refused to issue them land titles, they turned to the Mexican government to obtain valid land titles. They still continued to send representatives to the Arkansas Legislature. Richard Ellis, Samuel P. Carson, Robert Hamilton, Collin McKinney, and Albert H. Latimer represented Red River settlements at the Constitutional Convention at Washington-on-the-Brazos in 1836. Red River County was formally delineated by an act signed by President Sam Houston on December 14, 1837, during the First Congress of the Republic of Texas.

From the late 1830s until the War Between the States, Clarksville was the most important trading center in Northeast Texas. Steamboats brought goods from New Orleans by way of the Red River and delivered them to Rowland's Landing, which is 15 miles to the north. They were then hauled overland by wagon. During the 1850s, new steam sawmills and cotton gins added to the town's importance.

The first courthouse in Clarksville, a modest frame structure, was erected around 1840 in the center of the downtown square. The funds to build this building were raised by Isabella Clark Gordon, who sold the lots around the square in order to build the courthouse. In 1850, it was replaced by a larger red brick structure, and a brick jailhouse was built in 1852 on the 200 block on the north side of what is now West Main Street. Within a few years of the town's founding, numerous mercantile establishments opened on and around the square, and by the eve of the War Between the States, Clarksville's population had grown to around 900 people.

Clarksville's downtown square is typical of those throughout the southern part of the United States. Most of the buildings on the north side of the square were built in the 1870s and 1880s. When the old red brick courthouse was torn down, the look of the center of the square was changed. Several things stood in the center before the Confederate monument was erected in 1912, including a bandstand and a water well. The brick streets were put down around 1918. Of course, several large fires have plagued the square. Fire has twice destroyed the entire south side of the square. A fire in the late 1890s consumed half of the east side of the square. In the 1940s, a fire devastated the north half of the west side of the square, and in the 1950s, a fire engulfed the middle portion of the south side of the square.

Clarksville has been designated an official Texas Main Street City, as well as a National Main Street City and a Preserve American Community.

The Red River County Historical Society hopes that this photographic history will give a glimpse into the past of Clarksville and Red River County.

One

HISTORIC CLARKSVILLE SQUARE

This is the earliest known photograph of downtown Clarksville and was taken in 1863 looking east on Main Street. Of note is the rail fence around the Red River County courthouse, which was then located in the center of the square. There is snow on the ground, and horses are tied to the fence all around the courthouse. The area east of the square on East Main Street was known as "greasy row." (Courtesy of Eugene W. Bowers collection.)

On the west side of the Clarksville Square, the Donoho Hotel was built in 1842 by Captain William Donoho. This hotel was a noted stagecoach stop from 1842 until 1876, when the Texas and Pacific Railroad came to Clarksville. This photograph dates from the 1860s. The stagecoach that traveled between Clarksville and Little Rock had a beautiful lady painted on the door with the caption "The Belle of Clarksville" under it. (Courtesy of Eugene W. Bowers collection.)

In 1892, Gov. Jim Hogg visited Clarksville, arriving by carriage from the Texas and Pacific Depot. William Gordon is driving the open landau carriage and Governor Hogg is in the rear seat with his white hat prominent. On this visit, Isabella Clark Gordon (the wife of Clarksville's founder) presented Governor Hogg with an ornamental gourd that she had grown. He clutched the gourd to his chest, declaring that it was the finest gift he had ever received. While traveling on the train just west of town, he promptly threw the gourd from the window—onto her land, by coincidence. It was found, and from thenceforth, Hogg's name was "mud" in Clarksville. (Courtesy of Red River County Historical Society Collection, gift of Mildred Gordon Spencer.)

This view was taken from the tower of the Red River County Courthouse in March of 1892 facing south on Walnut Street. The two-story home in the foreground is the Swaim Boarding House. A derrick in the center of the square was erected to drill a water well, and the south side of the square is intact; it was destroyed by a second fire in the 1890s. (Courtesy of Red River County Historical Society Collection, gift of Ethel Stanley and Vera Stanley Smith.)

In March 1892, this photograph of the cotton yard near the Texas and Pacific Depot was taken north of the Red River County Courthouse. (Courtesy of Red River County Historical Society Collection, gift of Ethel Stanley and Vera Stanley Smith.)

This view was taken from the tower of the Red River County Courthouse in March of 1892 facing east. The two-story building is the Northern Standard Office, which was built in 1846. The Northern Standard Office was the first brick building built in Clarksville. The large building in front of the office is the Baptist Church, which was built in 1855. These buildings were on North Locust Street at the intersection of Madison Street. (Courtesy of Eugene W. Bowers collection.)

This view was taken from the tower of the Red River County Courthouse in March 1892 facing west. It shows the newly completed Red River County Jail (1887) and the expansion of Clarksville to the west along Main, Broadway, and Comanche Streets. (Courtesy of Red River County Historical Society Collection, gift of Ethel Stanley and Vera Stanley Smith.)

In 1891–1892, a new building was erected on the southeast corner of the square in order to house the First National Bank, which was founded in 1889. This impressive building lasted only eight years, burning in a great fire in 1900. The building was replaced by a less ornate building in 1901 that now houses the Chamber of Commerce. The DeFlorence Hotel was located behind the bank on East Main Street. (Courtesy of Eugene W. Bowers collection.)

The DeFlorence Hotel was constructed in 1893 east of the square on Main Street. This hotel was built after the Donoho Hotel was torn down and served those traveling on the Texas and Pacific Railroad. It also housed traveling actors, singers, and musicians who performed at the Trilling Opera House, which was located just to the east. A Venetian sky bridge connected the hotel to the opera house. (Courtesy of Eugene W. Bowers collection.)

In 1898, this photograph shows the southwest corner of the Clarksville Square at the intersection of West Main and Walnut Streets. (Courtesy of Eugene W. Bowers collection.)

Bray Brothers Millinery was a thriving business when this photograph was taken in 1898 on the east side of the Clarksville Square looking north along Locust Street. Well-dressed Victorian ladies would not appear in public without a hat, as this photograph depicts. (Courtesy of Eugene W. Bowers collection.)

Mud was always a problem before brick was placed on the square. Taken in 1898, this photograph shows the north side of the Clarksville Square and a wagon with its wheels covered with thick black mud. The newly built bandstand sits in the center of the square. (Courtesy of Eugene W. Bowers collection.)

A stylish couple is shown here crossing Main Street on the southeast corner of the Clarksville Square in 1898. Of particular note is the wooden walkway used to cross the muddy street. This view is looking south on Locust Street. (Courtesy of Eugene W. Bowers collection.)

The Red River National Bank was founded in 1874 as the Red River County Bank and was one of the oldest banks in the State of Texas. This building was erected in 1878 at the corner of North Walnut and Broadway Streets and is shown here in a 1910 photograph. The building was torn town in 1965. (Courtesy of Red River County Historical Society Collection.)

Watermelons have been raised on truck farms throughout Red River County from early days and were sold primarily on the Market Square. This 1910 photograph shows farmers selling their produce on the Clarksville Square looking south on Walnut Street. (Courtesy of Red River County Historical Society Collection.)

In the early part of the 20th century, a bandstand was erected in the center of the Clarksville Square to provide entertainment. This view is of the southeast corner of the square in 1910. (Courtesy of Red River County Historical Society Collection.)

A temperance parade was held in Clarksville in 1910 to promote the prohibition of alcohol. This scene is of the west side of the square looking south on Walnut Street. The Methodist Church spire may be seen in the background. (Courtesy of Red River County Historical Society Collection, gift of Dorothy Latimer Norwood.)

The City National Bank building was erected in 1911 at 200 West Main Street. During the Great Depression, the First National Bank bought the building and moved their operations here. A sign on the left of the building advertises the Marable Motor and Vehicle Company. (Courtesy of Red River County Historical Society Collection.)

In 1920, cars and wagons traveled equally on the streets of Clarksville, as this photograph depicts. A wagon turns west onto Main Street in front of the City National Bank, while a Ford Model A turns east onto Main Street. (Courtesy of Red River County Historical Society Collection.)

In 1930, a drawing was held to give away a free automobile, which was well attended by people from throughout Red River County. One of the stipulations was that you had to be present to win. While the winner's name has been lost, this photograph shows a packed crowd on the Clarksville Square waiting for the drawing. (Courtesy of Red River County Historical Society Collection.)

This view of the west side of Clarksville Square was taken in the early 1920s. (Courtesy of Red River County Historical Society Collection.)

This view of the north side of Clarksville Square was taken in the 1920s after the brick was installed around the square. (Courtesy of Eugene W. Bowers collection.)

This view of the south side of Clarksville Square was taken in the late 1920s. (Courtesy of Eugene W. Bowers collection.)

This view of the east side of Clarksville Square was taken in the late 1930s. (Courtesy of Eugene W. Bowers collection.)

The Avalon Theater was constructed on the south side of Clarksville Square in 1938 as one of the most modern theaters in Texas. The building is shown here in 1950. It was torn down in the late 1980s. (Courtesy of Red River County Historical Society Collection.)

This view of the northwest corner of Clarksville Square was taken in 1950 after the fire that destroyed the northern half of the west side of the square. (Courtesy of Red River County Historical Society Collection.)

This view of the southeast corner of Clarksville Square was taken in 1950. (Courtesy of Red River County Historical Society Collection.)

Two

KING COTTON

This view is the earliest photograph of cotton wagons in Clarksville's downtown and was taken of the northwest portion of the square in 1878. The Donoho Hotel is hidden behind the trees, and the newly constructed Red River National Bank is in the background. Cotton was brought from throughout the county to Clarksville after 1876 to be shipped on the Texas and Pacific Railroad. (Courtesy of Eugene W. Bowers collection.)

The R. T. Bryarly steamboat is shown here on the Red River. It was one of many steamboats that carried cotton from the port of Rowland on the Red River to Shreveport and on to New Orleans for sale. Prior to the coming of the railroad, this was the only means that cotton growers had to ship their product to market. Due to the ever-changing river conditions, cotton was not insured until it reached Shreveport, so there was great risk in the shipment of cotton. Bryarly operated a thriving port at Rowland until the coming of the railroad, at which time Rowland began to decline and is no longer in existence. (Courtesy of Lelia Bryarly Bonham Clark collection.)

This Bill of Lading is from a record book of cotton shipped from the Port of Rowland to New Orleans. This bill records 56 bales of cotton belonging to B. H. Epperson and bound for New Orleans in February of 1861. Each bale was marked to denote ownership, and the mark is recorded on the Bill of Lading. (Courtesy of Lelia Bryarly Bonham Clark collection.)

Shown here is a view of the southeast corner of the Clarksville Square taken in 1892. Each year, there was a prize given for the first bale of cotton brought to Clarksville. This view shows the elaborate original First National Bank building. The other businesses shown include Silberbergs, which originally was on the Red River at Rowland; Corley and Miesch Druggists; Shaws' Dry Goods; Harris Brothers; and the Barton and Murphy Drug Store. (Courtesy of Red River County Historical Society Collection.)

Shown here is the south side of the square in 1892. These buildings replaced wooden buildings, which burned in a great fire in 1878, destroying the entire south side. The Cotton Exchange Saloon was a thriving business, along with as many as seven other saloons. The spire of the Methodist Church is in the background. N. D. Trilling was an early merchant, and later his family operated the Trilling Opera House. Both the Latimer Brothers and N. B. Patton businesses sold dry goods and groceries. (Courtesy of Red River County Historical Society Collection.)

Cotton yards were primarily located along the Texas and Pacific Railroad tracks in Clarksville. After ginning, cotton was stored at cotton yards before being sent to the compress. This photograph was taken in 1892. Samples to grade the cotton were taken at the cotton yard by buyers to determine where the cotton would be shipped for ultimate sale. (Courtesy of Eugene W. Bowers collection.)

In 1908, this photograph was taken of cotton brought from a rural gin in Red River County. This view is on the north side of the Clarksville Square. This is early in the season and may be of the first bales brought to town. J. Ed Nichols, a prominent cotton buyer, is to the right of the wagon. It should be noted that the Star Grocery sold not only grocery and feed but whiskey too! (Courtesy of Eugene W. Bowers collection.)

In Red River County, 1910 was a banner year for the long staple cotton crop. Shown here is cotton sold by J. E. Proctor to local cotton buyer Collie Moore on October 3, 1910. The following people in the photograph are known: 1. Henry Lassiter, 2. J. Ed Nichols, 3. Collie Moore, 4. Sam Harris, 5. Archie Dick, and 6. Dave Hooks. (Courtesy of Red River County Historical Society Collection, gift of Joe Pinson.)

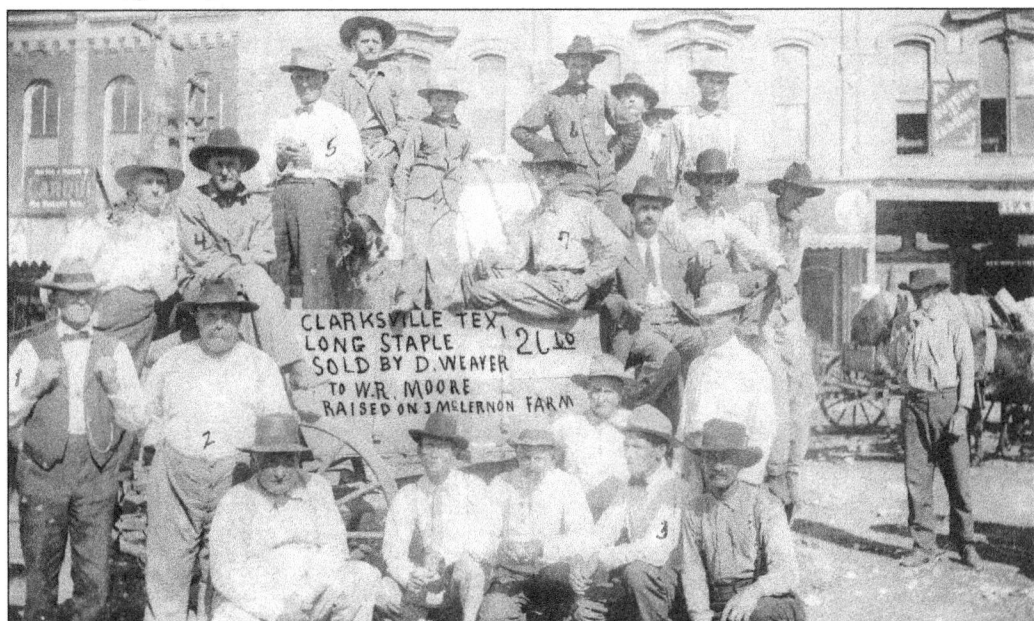

A prominent Clarksville cotton buyer, Will R. Moore purchased this cotton from D. Weaver for 26.60¢ per pound in 1910. The cotton was raised on the J. McLernon Farm. Those identified in the photograph are as follows: 1. J. Ed Nichols, 2. J. E. Proctor, 3. Sam Harris, 4. Denson Weaver, 5. Will R. Moore, 6. John McLernon, and 7. Henry Taylor. (Courtesy of Red River County Historical Society Collection, gift of Joe Pinson.)

Clarksville and Red River County long staple cotton was a very fine grade of cotton. Henry Taylor sold this cotton in 1910 for 25¢ per pound. Because of the fine grade of the cotton, prices of cotton on the Clarksville market were quoted at the Cotton Exchange in Dallas and as far away as New Orleans and New York City. (Courtesy of Red River County Historical Society Collection.)

Because of the popularity of the long staple cotton, exhibits were prepared to show the varieties of cotton grown in Red River County. This exhibit shows several of the types grown here at the Red River County Fair in 1913. (Courtesy of Red River County Historical Society Collection, gift of Dorothy Latimer Norwood.)

Ed Ferguson, who raised cotton on the Red River, sold three bales of his cotton to the partnership of J. Ed Nichols and D. I. Hooks in 1910 for 22–25¢ per pound. This view shows the southwest corner of the Clarksville Square. (Courtesy of Red River County Historical Society Collection, gift of Joe Pinson.)

Cotton was King in 1910 in Clarksville and Red River County, and lots of farms vied for the prize of the first bale, heaviest bale, and highest-grade bale. Shown here is a view in October 1910 of the northeast corner of the square. Just as today, businesses came and went from year to year, often dependent upon the cotton crop of the year. (Courtesy of Red River County Historical Society Collection.)

These bales of cotton were sold by Ed Ferguson to Rosco Johnson on October 19, 1910, for 30¢ per pound, which was a very high price. This view is up north Walnut Street past the old Red River National Bank. After sales on the square, cotton was taken up Walnut Street to the various cotton yards for storage. The mud on this street was often a problem, and the story goes that one fall a mule drowned in the deep mud in the middle of Walnut Street. (Courtesy of Red River County Historical Society Collection.)

A particularly high grade of cotton was grown on Peter's Prairie, which is southeast of Clarksville. Shown here are young women picking cotton to be taken to the gin in 1910. Often times, a particular plot would be set aside for a church or social club and then the proceeds of the sale of the cotton given to that group. (Courtesy of Red River County Historical Society Collection.)

With the coming of the automobile, fewer and fewer wagons brought the cotton to town, and trucks with cotton trailers replaced them. This view in the early 1920s is of the southwest corner of the square after the erection of the Confederate monument in 1917 and the construction of the City National Bank on the southwest corner of the square. (Courtesy of Red River County Historical Society Collection.)

A series of postcards was made in the 1910s depicting various cotton scenes in and around Clarksville. This card brags about the high cotton prices in Clarksville and the size of the bolls. (Courtesy of Red River County Historical Society Collection.)

The weighing of the cotton was a very important event in the lives of all cotton farmers. Shown here are two small boys in Clarksville after the weighing of bales in the 1920s. (Courtesy of Red River County Historical Society Collection.)

These four gentlemen are shown weighing a bale of cotton, which was sold to one of the many cotton brokers in Clarksville. The official "cotton weigher" was a very important job, and at one time, this was an elected position voted on by the people of Clarksville. Each community had its own elected official cotton weigher. (Courtesy of Red River County Historical Society Collection.)

In 1899, Jake Gaffney was named honorary "Sheriff for the Day" because he picked the most pounds of cotton for the season. Jake, who picked cotton on a farm on the Red River, is shown here on the south side of the square after being elected to his high office. This was a much vied for award and was only achieved after much hard work. (Courtesy of Red River County Historical Society Collection, gift of Joe Pinson.)

Jake Gaffney is shown here with his sherriff's posse after being named "Sheriff for the Day" in 1899. Those in the photograph are: 1. Henry Latimer, 2. Silas Rose, 3. Charlie Terry, 4. Collie Moore, 5. Ed Nichols, 6. Jake Gaffney, 7. John Wright, 8. George Moody, 9. Bob Lassiter, 10. James Aubrey, 11. Frank Owens, 12. Archie Dick, 13. Jim Moore, 14. Harvey Jones, 15. Bill Dugan, 16. John Beeson, 17. David Hooks, 18. Rosco Johnson, 19. Tom Hankins, 20. John Webb, 21. Sam Harris, 22. Sheb Gabbert, and 23. Will Moore. (Courtesy of Red River County Historical Society Collection, gift of Joe Pinson.)

Three cotton yards were in Clarksville, with this one being located north of the Texas and Pacific Railroad tracks. (Courtesy of Red River County Historical Society Collection.)

The Annona Cotton Yard was located near the Texas and Pacific Railroad. The coming of the railroad in 1876 dramatically changed the cotton market in Red River County and allowed for the easy and safe shipment of this important commodity. (Courtesy of Red River County Historical Society Collection.)

This cotton yard was located north of the Texas and Pacific Railroad tracks. The cotton compress is shown in the background. (Courtesy of Red River County Historical Society Collection.)

This cotton yard was located south of the Texas and Pacific Railroad tracks and west of the compress. (Courtesy of Red River County Historical Society Collection.)

At the Annona Fair in 1915, the E. K. Russell Cotton Farm had an exhibit that spelled out "Russell" with its large bolls and displayed its varieties of cotton grown. Joe Pope is shown with the exhibit. (Courtesy of E. K. Russell Sr. family collection.)

E. K. Russell's cotton, grown in the Kickapoo Bottom, which was south of Annona, is shown in this photograph. Russell grew a variety of cotton known as "Russell's Big Boll Cotton." (Courtesy of E. K. Russell Sr. family collection.)

The Scaff Gin was located west of Clarksville in the Batesville Community. Most communities in Red River County had small gins where the cotton was ginned before being taken to Clarksville for sale and shipment. (Courtesy of Red River County Historical Society, gift of Georgia Swann Van Dyke Fowler.)

The National Cotton Compress was located on the south side of the Texas and Pacific Railroad tracks at the intersection of North Cedar and Depot Streets. In the fall, the compress worked 24 hours a day, 7 days a week to compress the cotton. This was a huge facility that employed many people during the season. Bill Bettes Sr. was the longtime manager of the facility. It was torn down in the 1970s. (Courtesy of Red River County Historical Society Collection.)

The Clarksville Cotton Seed Oil Mill was located east of the Texas and Pacific Railroad depot. The plant used the seed from the cotton and incorporated it into cattle feed. The aroma from the plant could be smelled all over town during milling season. Pat Graves and later Peyton West served as managers of the oil mill. As is evidenced, cotton created its own economy through various industries in the county. (Courtesy of Red River County Historical Society Collection, gift of Audrey Graves Black.)

Three

HISTORIC HOMES

The original part of the DeMorse Home was built by Isaac Smathers in 1833 as a two-room log cabin and was the first home built in Clarksville. Smathers lived in the home until 1842, when Charles DeMorse purchased it and added to the home. The home is located at 105 East Comanche Street. This photograph is c. 1948 and shows Isabella DeMorse Latimer, DeMorse's granddaughter, peering through the window. (Courtesy of Red River County Historical Society Collection.)

In 1936, the Texas Centennial Commission placed a marker in the front lawn of the house to mark the significance of both DeMorse and his newspaper *The Standard* as being one of the oldest newspapers in the State of Texas. DeMorse collected plant specimens and bulbs to add to his flower garden, which was widely acclaimed. (Courtesy of Red River County Historical Society Collection.)

Charles DeMorse was somewhat of an Anglophile and wished for his home to look like an English country home. As such, he added clapboard to the log cabin and English chimney pots and connected the detached kitchen to the home, as this 1950 photograph shows. (Courtesy of Red River County Historical Society Collection.)

In 1833, the town's founders, James and Isabella Clark, built the second home in Clarksville. Like the DeMorse Home, it started as a log cabin and grew to this two-story home. The home was located on East Broadway and east of the present St. Joseph Catholic Church. The home burned in 1910. (Courtesy of Clark family collection.)

This home was built by John Monkhouse in the Walnut Grove community on the Red River, which was north of Clarksville prior to the War Between the States. The home was occupied by many families throughout its history and tragically burned in the 1980s. (Courtesy of Elmer Bentsen family collection.)

This photograph dates from the 1880s and pictures an antebellum home on North Columbia Street in Clarksville, directly east of the DeMorse Home. This home burned in 2008. (Courtesy of Red River County Historical Society Collection.)

The antebellum McKenzie Home was located southwest of Clarksville on the campus of the McKenzie College. McKenzie descendants occupied the home until the 1960s. Sadly, the home burned in the 1980s. (Courtesy of Anne Russell Evetts collection.)

Shown here is the home of Charley and Mattie Spike, which was built soon after the War Between the States, on the 600 block of North Walnut Street in Clarksville. Mattie (left) is shown in this photograph with an unidentified woman. Charley went off to seek his fortune in the Alaska Gold Rush. Unfortunately, he was lost at sea en route. She always kept a light burning in the window in hope that he would some day return. (Courtesy of Eugene W. Bowers collection.)

Edward S. and Sue Belle VanDyke Chambers built this home on South Lafayette Street in the 1870s. Judge Chambers served as district judge at the Red River County Courthouse. (Courtesy of Clark Family collection.)

E. M. and Josie Teel Bowers occupied this home, which was built in the 1870s on North Walnut Street on the east side of the 700 block. E. M. Bowers' father, Will, was an early day carpenter and built many homes in Clarksville. (Courtesy of Eugene W. Bowers collection.)

Otto Glosnop came to Clarksville with the Union Army of Occupation following the War Between the States. He was an expert woodworker and craftsman. He built this home for Dr. Look. The home was later occupied by Mr. and Mrs. Newt Grigsby and then by their daughter Lelia and her husband, Seth King. (Courtesy of Red River County Historical Society Collection.)

Albert and Lela Martin Wooley's home was located just north of Clarksville. The home was built in the 1890s. The Wooley daughters—Lela May, Lucille, Christine, and Mildred—remembered how drafty the home was in the winter, but cool summer breezes blew through the house in hot weather. The home is shown here in a 1940s photograph. (Courtesy of Lela May Wooley Beadle collection.)

The home of Dr. Preston Hocker is shown in this photograph. The home was an elaborate Victorian structure on the 600 block of West Main Street in Clarksville. Today the Red River Motor Bank is located there. It was built around 1895. In the 1970s, the entire home was moved to Fort Worth, where it has been beautifully restored. (Courtesy of Sam Lennox Hocker collection.)

The home of Charles David and Sallie Bagby Lennox is shown here soon after it was built in 1897. Shown here are, from left to right, daughter Rannie and sons Bagby and David. This home at 601 West Broadway has stood the test of time and has been beautifully restored. It now serves as the headquarters of the Red River County Historical Society. (Courtesy of Red River County Historical Society Collection.)

After studying architecture at Columbia University in New York, Bagby Lennox made changes to the home in 1916, including adding a sun room, an upstairs sleeping porch, a portochere, and moving the front door. (Courtesy of Red River County Historical Society Collection.)

Shown here is a photograph of the C. D. Lennox house as it looked in the 1960s. (Courtesy of Red River County Historical Society Collection.)

This close-up shows the fine details of the C. D. Lennox home during a winter snowfall in the 1960s. (Courtesy of Red River County Historical Society Collection.)

The F. F. and Mattie Corley Marable home, which stood on the 1000 block of West Main Street, is show here. The front stairs had seven steps—one for each child, who were Ben, Paul, Ruth, Mary, Susie, F. F. Jr., and Carrie. The home was torn down in the late 1950s. (Courtesy of Marable family collection.)

This home at 909 West Broadway is shown in a 1942 photograph with J. W. and Evelyn Nichols in the yard along with their young son John. The home was built in the 1890s, and prior to the Nichols' ownership, the C. E. Williams family owned it. (Courtesy of John M. Nichols collection.)

E. K. Russell Sr. built this home northwest of Annona c. 1900. Russell was a prominent cotton grower and active in Red River County politics. He ran for governor in 1934. The home burned in 2007. (Courtesy of Anne Russell Evetts collection.)

The Wren Boarding House served travelers for over 40 years, as well as serving meals to local residents. It was located on the northeast corner of North Locust and Monroe Streets in Clarksville. (Courtesy of Richard D. "Dick" Wren collection.)

The First Presbyterian Church manse was built in 1905 on the same block of the church, which was to the west. The McKenzie Methodist Church spire is shown in the background, and Dr. Samuel Templeton is shown in front of the manse in this photograph. The home served ministers until the mid-1960s, when a new manse was built. (Courtesy of First Presbyterian Church Collection.)

The Clarence Hocker home, on the 600 block of West Main Street, was one of Clarksville's most impressive homes. The home was built in 1910 but was burned after being struck by lightning some years later. (Courtesy of Red River County Historical Society Collection.)

Morgan and Hallie Graves built this grand home at 100 East College Avenue in 1905, with the third floor serving as a ballroom. An ornate iron fence and immaculate grounds and gardens surrounded the home. Morgan Graves was the president of the Red River National Bank and served as president of the Texas Bankers Association. The home burned in the 1940s after a gas explosion. (Courtesy of Eugene W. Bowers collection.)

Mr. and Mrs. H. H. Lennox built this home in 1916 in the Georgian style. The home features three floors, as well as a basement. The home has had numerous owners and is still one of Clarksville's most impressive homes. (Courtesy of Red River County Historical Society Collection.)

This home at 1206 South Locust in Clarksville was built by Clovis Graves in the 1910s, which was when this section of town was still in the country. Graves is shown here in his automobile in front of the home. This home remains today in beautiful condition, and one is reminded of the grand days of the past. (Courtesy of Red River County Historical Society Collection.)

This colonial revival home was owned by the O'Neill Family and was located on the 500 block of West Main Street in Clarksville. The home was occupied by the family for many years and was later an apartment house. It was torn down in the 1950s. (Courtesy of Red River County Historical Society Collection.)

Charles and Essie Grant Walker built this prairie-style home at 601 West Main Street in the 1910s. The home was the scene of much social activity for many years. It was torn down in the 1970s. (Courtesy of Eugene W. Bowers collection.)

This home was built by Paul Ussery in the 1930s at 1011 West Jackson Street, which was part of a new section of Clarksville that was known as Hocker Heights. Pat C. and Lela May Wooley Beadle occupied the home for many years. (Courtesy of Beadle family collection.)

This home at 901 West Broadway was built by Will and Nellie Donoho Hamilton. Nellie was a well-known Clarksville hostess and entertained with great parties in the home. Will was a longtime merchant on the north side of the downtown square. (Courtesy of Red River County Historical Society Collection.)

The photograph shows the interior of the Hamilton Home with the Hamiltons in the dining room. This was taken around 1905 and is an example of a stylish young couple's home. (Courtesy of Red River County Historical Society Collection.)

Four

1914 COUNTY FAIR
PARADE AND RACETRACK

In 1913, the Red River County Fair Association, under the leadership of county agent Will McMaster, organized and purchased land west of Clarksville near the intersection of the present day US 82 and SH 37. Prior to this time, the first Red River County Fair was organized in 1856 and was called the Red River County Agricultural and Mechanical Association. The War Between the States brought an end to this organization. This photograph shows the grandstand at the racetrack where horse races were held. The grandstand was said to have had a seating capacity of 1,200 people. This chapter will show the elaborate cars, buggies, and floats that participated in a parade for the fair in 1914. (Courtesy of Red River County Historical Society Collection.)

Shown on the east side of the Clarksville Square, these two ladies are resplendent in white in their buggy with a matching pair of white horses. The parade began downtown, circling the square and then proceeding to the fairgrounds to mark the official start of the fair. (Courtesy of Red River County Historical Society Collection.)

Mrs. A. M. (Hallie Dick) Graves is shown here in her buggy decorated with chrysanthemums. She was the grand dame of Clarksville society during this era. Her husband was the president of the Red River National Bank. This view is on the south side of the Clarksville Square. (Courtesy of Red River County Historical Society Collection.)

Capt. A. P. Dick is shown here in his daughter Hallie Graves' buggy before the parade. Captain Dick served in the Army of the Confederacy and was a well-known Clarksville citizen. (Courtesy of Red River County Historical Society Collection.)

Mrs. Bill (Della) Bettes Sr. is shown here in her surrey with two young ladies. Della's husband was the manager of the Clarksville Cotton Compress. Della never drove a car. (Courtesy of Red River County Historical Society Collection.)

Louise Cheatham (left) and Zella (Hocker) Teel are shown here in their carriage with the west side of the Clarksville Square in the background. (Courtesy of Red River County Historical Society Collection.)

The Clarksville Steam Laundry was represented in the parade by their delivery wagon. The north side of the Clarksville Square is in the background. (Courtesy of Red River County Historical Society Collection.)

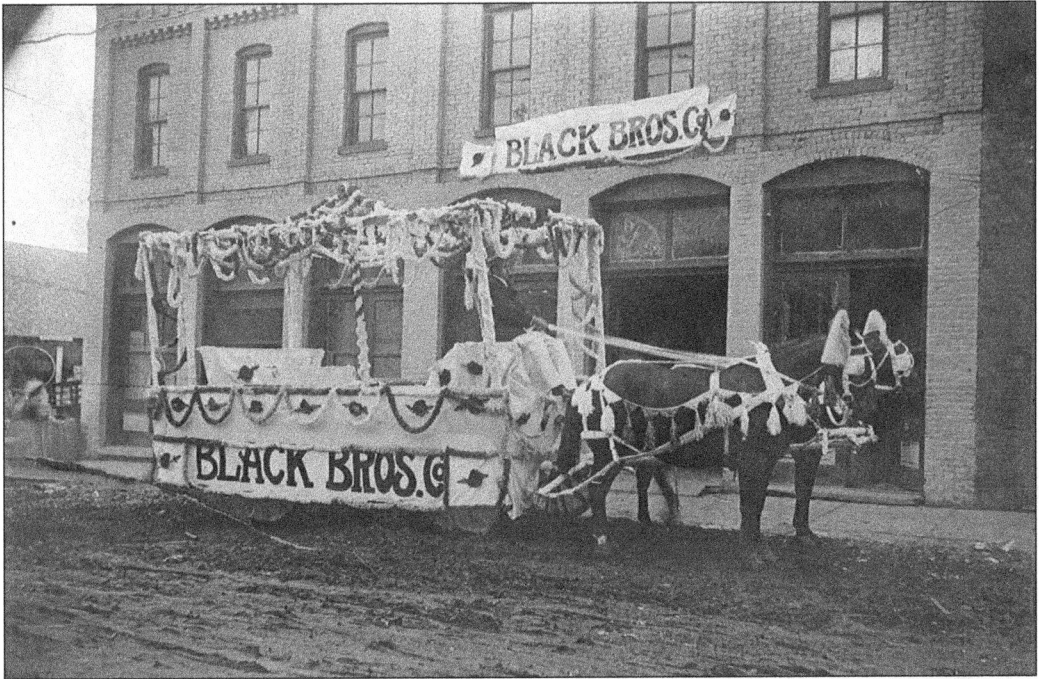

The float for the Black Brothers Company, run by Ernest P. and Eugene Black, is shown here in front of their business on East Main Street. (Courtesy of Red River County Historical Society Collection.)

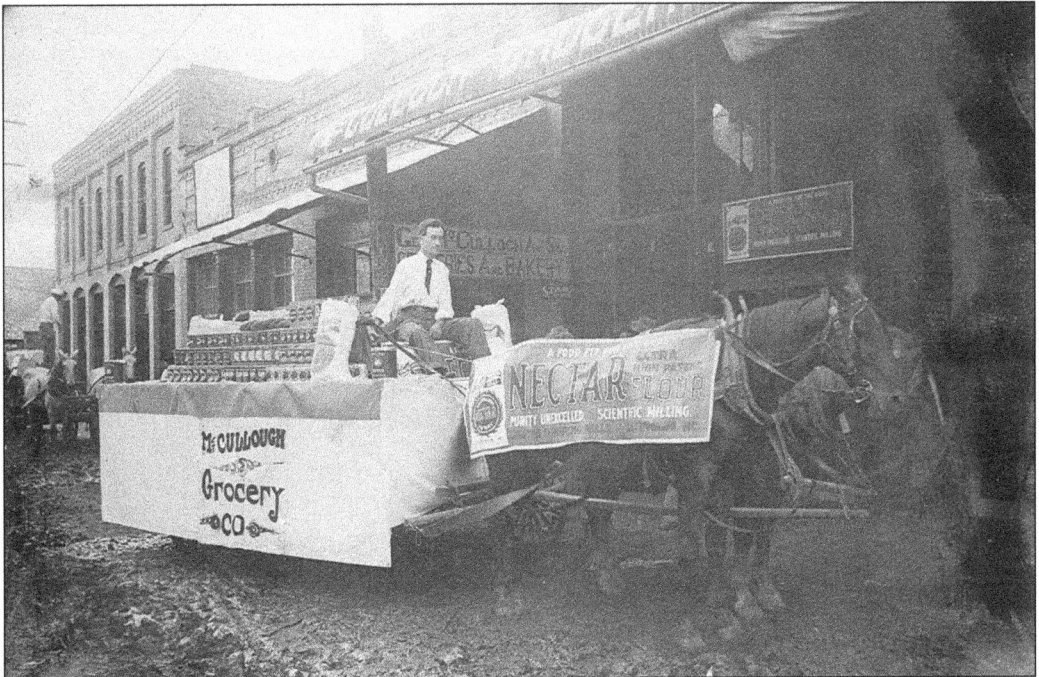

Charles McDonald is shown here on the George McCulloch and Son Grocery and Bakery float in front of their business on East Main Street, which is where the *Clarksville Times* office is now located. (Courtesy of Red River County Historical Society Collection.)

This float had a theme of "Beginning the Voyage" and represented different colleges and universities that local students were attending at the time. (Courtesy of Red River County Historical Society Collection.)

The Collin County Mill and Elevator Company's entry is shown here. Longtime Clarksville teacher Rosine (Dickson) Bagby is one of the young ladies on the float. (Courtesy of Red River County Historical Society Collection.)

The D. D. Strong Dry Goods float is shown here. The business was located on the west side of the square at that time. Adele O'Neill Baker is one of the young ladies on the float along with the driver, Robert Cook. (Courtesy of Red River County Historical Society Collection.)

Local agricultural products are shown on this float, which obviously included corn and hay. The west side of the square is shown in the background. (Courtesy of Red River County Historical Society Collection.)

The Graves and Johnson Grocery and Bakery float is shown here with Pat Graves, the owner, in the suit. His daughter, Audrey (Graves) Black, is riding along (second child from the left). Graves and Johnson was located at the south end of the west side of the square. (Courtesy of Red River County Historical Society Collection.)

Henry and Smith Brothers float is shown here representing LaFrance Flour, which was touted to be the "Best Flour on Earth." (Courtesy of Red River County Historical Society Collection.)

F. F. Marable Sr., along with some of his children, is shown here driving the float for his store, Marable Hardware Company. This retail establishment was located on West Main Street just west of the square and sold fine hardware, including the most modern ranges, heating stoves, firearms, china, and crystal. (Courtesy of Red River County Historical Society Collection.)

The most modern cook stoves are shown here in the Majestic Range float entry. The west side of the square is in the background. (Courtesy of Red River County Historical Society Collection.)

This float shows a pet Hereford steer along with sacks of cottonseed cake feed that was made at the Clarksville Oil Mill. (Courtesy of Red River County Historical Society Collection.)

These young men belong to a local brass band that played for the parade. The band was conducted by Lee Hoy of Bonham and led the parade. For the occasion, Hoy composed a march called "The Clarksville Times March." Clarksville had several brass bands that played for many dances that were held during this time. (Courtesy of Red River County Historical Society Collection.)

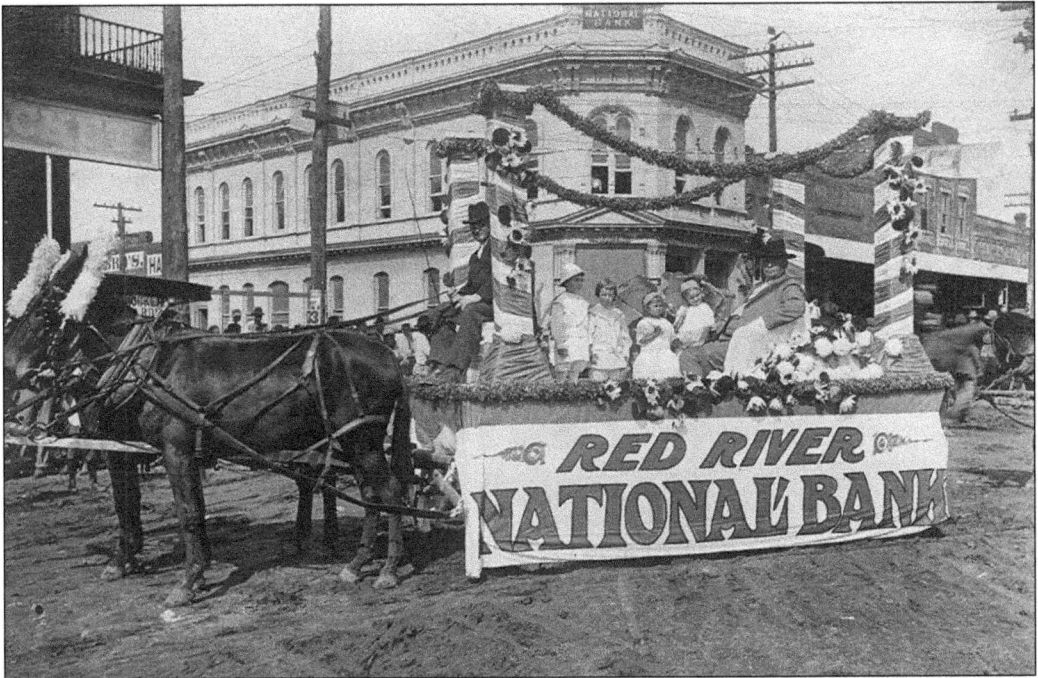

Dr. Ballard Dinwiddie is shown here along with several young ladies on the Red River National Bank float in front of the bank on the northwest corner of the square. (Courtesy of Red River County Historical Society Collection.)

Clarence and Hattie Hocker are shown here in their new automobile (with the driver on the right) along with daughters Dorothy, Zella, and Edith. (Courtesy of Red River County Historical Society Collection.)

Genevieve Butcher (driving), whose husband, Bernard, owned the Butcher Drug Company on the north side of the square, is shown here with her daughter Edith and friends. (Courtesy of Red River County Historical Society Collection.)

This stylish automobile was used to advertise the annual Confederate Reunion. (Courtesy of Red River County Historical Society Collection.)

This elaborately decorated automobile is shown with Edith Durrum driving and Margaret (Bowers) Milan in the backseat, far left, along with their friends. (Courtesy of Red River County Historical Society Collection.)

This early white automobile is festively decorated in all white with flowers and streamers. Unfortunately, the occupants are unidentified. (Courtesy of Red River County Historical Society Collection.)

The grandstand at the Clarksville Racetrack is shown here awaiting the beginning of the next race. At night, great fireworks displays were held to entertain the crowds, and cars parked in the infield of the track to watch these displays. (Courtesy of Red River County Historical Society Collection.)

As is evident, huge crowds attended the horse races during the annual fair. The crowd is watching an air show where Art Smith and his airplane performed between races in this photograph. The pilot of the plane was sued by a farmer in Kansas because his plane had frightened several of his cows and caused them to produce less milk! (Courtesy of Red River County Historical Society Collection.)

Five

Historic County Courthouse

This is the invitation to the opening of the new Red River County Courthouse at 400 North Walnut Street in Clarksville in 1885. This was the third courthouse to be built in Clarksville, with the two previous buildings being located in the center of the downtown square. The building was built at a cost of $60,000, and the first trial was held in November 1885. (Courtesy of Eugene W. Bowers collection.)

This view is of the second courthouse, which was in the center of the Clarksville Square and was built in 1859. The building was made of red brick and stood until 1885, which was when it was torn down. (Courtesy of Red River County Historical Society Collection.)

This photograph was taken on September 10, 1885, the opening day of the new Red River County Courthouse, and was taken from North Walnut Street. (Courtesy of Eugene W. Bowers collection.)

This invitation is to a grand ball that was given by the citizens of Clarksville to honor the Red River Rifles, a group of local militiamen, at the Red River County Courthouse in September of 1890. (Courtesy of Clark family collection.)

Grand + Ball + and + Banquet,

GIVEN BY THE CITIZENS OF CLARKSVILLE TO THE

RED RIVER RIFLES,

—AT THE—

Court House, Clarksville, Texas,

ON THE NIGHT OF

SEPTEMBER 19, 1890.

You are most cordially invited to be present.

✳ ✳ ✳ COMMITTEES: ✳ ✳ ✳

ON INVITATION:

LIEUT. COL. M. S. SWAIN,   DR. C. T. CLARK,   H. B. WRIGHT, ESQ.
GUS. SHAW, ESQ.,   HOWARD DICK,   HENRY DICKSON.

ON RECEPTION:

MR. AND MRS. J. C. MYERS,   MR. AND MRS. WILL TAYLOR,
MR. AND MRS. D. W. CHEATHAM,   MR. AND MRS. R. B. EPPERSON,
MR. AND MRS. H. L. NORRIS,   MR. AND MRS. J. B. LASSITER.

ON ARRANGEMENTS:

W. W. WARD,   WILL TAYLOR,   JNO. GORDON,
HOWARD BROWN,   MORGAN GRAVES,   ALBERT BETTES.

FLOOR MANAGERS:

J. W. McCULLOCH,   H. L. NORRIS,   W. W. WARD,
    HENRY DICKSON,   JNO. S GORDON

This 1910 view of the Red River County Courthouse was taken from the north side of Walnut Street and shows the 1910 addition to the far left. This photograph shows how the trees have matured in just 30 years. (Courtesy of Red River County Historical Society Collection.)

This panoramic view of the Red River County Courthouse was taken in the early 1930s looking north on Walnut Street. On the far left is Dr. Lucius Pearson's dental office, with the courthouse in the center and the Clarksville Post Office on the far right, which was completed in 1914. (Courtesy of Red River County Historical Society Collection.)

This photograph was taken in 1939 from the corner of Cedar and Madison Streets. The domino table may be seen between the two trees to the far right. (Courtesy of Red River County Historical Society Collection.)

This interior view of the courthouse was taken in 1955 and shows the judge's bench on the west side of the courtroom. The judge's bench was moved from the east end in 1910 due to the noise level of the traffic on North Walnut Street. (Courtesy of Red River County Historical Society Collection.)

In the 1950s, a series of postcards was made with scenes in Clarksville. This view is from the south side of the Red River County Courthouse. (Courtesy of Red River County Historical Society Collection.)

This is a view of the Red River County Courthouse taken in the late 1950s from the south side. (Courtesy of Red River County Historical Society Collection.)

Six

HISTORIC CLARKSVILLE CHURCHES

The First Presbyterian Church in Clarksville, founded in 1833, is recognized as the oldest Protestant congregation in continuous service in Texas. This is the congregation's first building in Clarksville, and it was located where the current building now stands, at the corner of Main and Pecan Streets. It was built in 1859 on the banks of the Delaware and served the congregation until 1890. (Courtesy of First Presbyterian Church Collection.)

This was the second building to house the congregation of the First Presbyterian Church in Clarksville. The building was constructed in 1890 and burned in a thunderstorm in 1904. (Courtesy of First Presbyterian Church Collection.)

In 1938, the choir of the First Presbyterian Church was featured in an article in *The Dallas Morning News* and this photograph was used. Those in the photograph, from left to right, are (first row) Ruth Reed McCulloch (Organist), Mary Kennedy, Katie Bell Fowler Hutchison, Abbie Latimer, Marian Duncan, Mollie Banks Sloan, Janice Holloway, Ruth Marable (Director), Katherine Shadid Smiley, Ione Fowler Chambliss, Susie Marable, and Wilson Cole (Minister); (second row) Charles Anderson, Forrest West, M. D. Vaughan, Ritchie McCulloch, F. F. "Son" Marable Jr., Frank Upchurch, and Pat Graves. (Courtesy of First Presbyterian Church Collection.)

The current building of the First Presbyterian Church was completed in 1905, with additions made in 1917 and 1930. This beautiful sanctuary is still in use by the congregation today. (Courtesy of First Presbyterian Church Collection.)

In June 1933, the First Presbyterian Church celebrated its 100th anniversary with special services and a picnic on the grounds. Longtime members and former ministers were honored. Those pictured, from left to right, include the following: (first row) Mrs. George McCulloch, The. Reverend H. R. Hogan. The Reverend L. P. Parker, Morgan Latimer, The Reverend Sam Templeton, The Reverend J. C. Hollyman, Jap Dinwwidie, John Barry, A. H. Latimer, Mrs. Joe Darnell, Mrs. Ed Bloodworth, Lucy Roberts, Mrs. Will Taylor, and Mrs. John Bagby; (second row) Will Taylor, Milton Harris, Mrs. Albert Fall, Della Jolley, Bonnie Patton, Ida Dysart, Sallie Lennox, John A. Bagby, Walker Hopkins, Malcolm Hopkins, C. D. Lennox, Mrs. J. Q. Mehaffey, Mattie Corley Marable, Mrs. Wade Parks, Jap Barry, Henry Latimer, Imogene Moore, Morgan Graves, Joe Darnell, and R. M. White. (Courtesy of First Presbyterian Church Collection.)

M. E. CHURCH. SOUTH. CLARKSVILLE. TEXAS

The McKenzie Memorial United Methodist Church was founded in 1838 and is one of the oldest Methodist congregations in Texas. This building was erected in 1901 at the corner of West Broadway and Pecan Streets in Clarksville, which replaced a structure located at the corner of Washington Avenue and South Walnut Street. This photograph was taken in 1910. This imposing structure served the congregation for 75 years and was torn down in 1976. (Courtesy of Red River County Historical Society Collection.)

This view of the McKenzie Methodist Church was taken in 1948 before the bell tower was removed and shows the addition of the Sunday school buildings. (Courtesy of Red River County Historical Society Collection.)

The interior of the McKenzie Methodist Church, decorated for a wedding, is shown in this 1960 photograph. (Courtesy of Red River County Historical Society Collection.)

The Men's Sunday School Class of McKenzie Methodist Church is shown in this 1925 photograph. Those in the photograph, from left to right, include the following: (first row) Ross Hughston, L. W. Pope, Will Mehaffey, and the remainder unidentified; (second row) W. N. Birkhead, unidentified, and O. W. McBride; (third row) E. P. Black, Sam Ferguson, Clarence Hocker, Dick Lawrence, Josh Brindley, Otis Hocker, unidentified, Dr. E. M. Smith, J. A. Dysart, and Robert Mehaffey; (fourth row) John Ward, Gordon McCulloch, Gaston Muns, Walter S. Richmond, and Charlie Carter; (fifth row) Tom Williams, J. W. Shackleford, A. B. Mauldin, M. M. White, unidentified, O. B. Baker, Gilbert Gaines, J. R. Tucker, Brother Graham, D. D. Strong, T. B. Miller, Hugh Chain, and unidentified. (Courtesy of Red River County Historical Society Collection.)

Shown here is the First Baptist Church in Clarksville, which was built in 1905. This congregation was established in 1845. This structure replaced their building on North Locust Street. This building was located on South Walnut Street at Taylor Streets and was torn down in 1959. (Courtesy of Red River County Historical Society Collection.)

St. Joseph's Catholic Church was founded in 1860, with this building being built in 1872 on East Main Street. The building is shown here in a 1925 photograph with the cemetery fence in the foreground. This building was destroyed by fire in 1930. (Courtesy of St. Joseph Catholic Church Collection.)

This photograph is of St. Joseph's second building, which was built in 1930 and torn down in the 1980s. (Courtesy of St. Joseph Catholic Church Collection.)

The First Christian Church (Disciples of Christ) was founded in 1883. Their original church building was located on Broadway Street, two blocks east of the square. This building was built in 1932 and continues to serve the congregation. (Courtesy of Red River County Historical Society Collection.)

The St. John Lutheran Church congregation was founded in 1912 and purchased this building from the Old School Presbyterian congregation. The building was located on South Walnut Street and is shown in this 1932 photograph with a 1927 Ford Model T in front. (Courtesy of St. John Lutheran Church Collection.)

Members of St. John Lutheran Church pictured in 1935, from left to right, include the following: (first row) Wesley Schumacher, Bobby Eilers, Charles Dillman, Curtis Bachman, Bobby Hoeldtke, Herman Hausler, and Erick Hausler; (second row) Henrietta Edzards, Otto Edzards, John Edzards, Ernest Bachman, Henry Spoede, Louis Bachman, Franklin Eilers, Adolph Hausler, Henry Bachman, and George Banke; (third row) Ruby Hoeldtke, Frank Eilers, Lorene Dillman, Charles Dillman, Otto Adrian, Art Schumacher, Otto Hoeldtke, Fred Banke, Fred Hausler, Ernest Hoeldtke, Reverend Smith's father, Charles Hoeldtke, and Freddie Eilers. (Courtesy of St. John Lutheran Church Collection.)

The ladies of St. John Lutheran Church pictured in 1935, from left to right, include the following: (first row) Frances Schumacher, Della Hausler, Dorothy Bachman with Yvonne Smith in front, Mary Edzards, Alvena Spoede, Barbara Schumacher, and Elaine Adrian; (second row) Clara Hausler, Elizabeth Bachman, Ella Bachman, Gertrude Hausler, Carrie Bachman, Mayme Eilers, Flora Edzards, Emilia Edzards, and Henrietta Edzards; (third row) Martha Dillman, Esther Schumacher, Matilda Spoede, Elma Adrian, Alice Bachman, Gladys Eilers, Minie Edzards, Antye Edzards, and Ruby Hoeldtke. (Courtesy of St. John Lutheran Church Collection.)

Christ Church, Episcopal was founded as a mission by the Episcopal Diocese of Dallas and was the oldest congregation in the diocese. This building at 501 West Main Street was built in 1927 and served the congregation through the 1980s, when it was given to the Red River County Historical Society. (Courtesy of Red River County Historical Society Collection.)

The Clarksville Church of Christ on the 1000 block of West Main Street is shown in this 1950 photograph. (Courtesy of Red River County Historical Society Collection.)

Seven

HISTORIC BUILDINGS AND BUSINESSES

The *Clarksville Times* was founded in 1873, and this photograph was taken of the interior of their offices in 1890. These offices burned soon after in 1893. The *Times* has been in continuous business since it was founded and is the oldest business establishment in Red River County. (Courtesy of Red River County Historical Society Collection.)

The Clarksville Canning Company employees are shown in this 1892 photograph. The company canned local vegetables and was located north of the Texas and Pacific Railroad tracks in Clarksville. (Courtesy of Eugene W. Bowers collection.)

CARNEGIE LIBRARY, CLARKSVILLE, TEXAS.

The Carnegie Library was located at 505 West Main Street in Clarksville and was built in 1902 at a cost of $10,000. The library closed in 1907 after the City of Clarksville withdrew its financial support. The building later served as a home, hotel, and law offices before burning in the late 1970s. (Courtesy of Red River County Historical Society Collection.)

The Clarksville Opera House replaced the Trilling Opera House after it burned. This building was the scene of many theatrical productions and musical programs. After closing as an opera house, the building housed a movie theater known as the Utagrand. The roof of the building collapsed during a storm in 1935 and was torn down soon thereafter. (Courtesy of Red River County Historical Society Collection.)

The interior of the Clarksville Opera House is shown in this photograph taken c. 1925. Large productions were held here, as is evidenced by this photograph. (Courtesy of Red River County Historical Society Collection.)

Shown here in an 1882 photograph is the Gaffney and Briggance Store (second from the left) located in Opah, Texas, which was a community north of Clarksville on the Red River. The community caved into the river in 1910. (Courtesy of Clark family collection.)

The Black Brothers Company was founded in 1898 by Ernest P. and Eugene Black. One of their wagons is shown here loaded with slabs of bacon on the north side of the Clarksville Square in 1915. (Courtesy of Red River County Historical Society Collection.)

The Black Brothers Company building is shown in this photograph on East Main Street. Black Brothers was one of the earliest bottlers of Coca-Cola in Texas and had their own brand of soda pop known as Mission drinks. E. P. Black is shown on the far left of this photograph along with other employees. (Courtesy of Red River County Historical Society Collection.)

Black Brothers Wholesale Grocery employees are shown in their delivery truck in this photograph. They delivered groceries and supplies to many small grocery stores in rural areas of Red River County. (Courtesy of Red River County Historical Society Collection.)

The D. D. Strong Dry Goods is shown in this 1910 photograph. The store was located on the west side of the Clarksville Square in the middle of the block. (Courtesy of Red River County Historical Society Collection.)

Shown here is the interior of the Kunkel and Dysart Grocery Company. John G. Kunkel and J. A. Dysart, the owners, are in the center of the photograph. (Courtesy of Red River County Historical Society Collection.)

Hamilton Dry Goods is shown in this 1902 photograph. The store was known to have the finest quality dry goods. Will and Nellie Donoho Hamilton owned the store. Those pictured are, from left to right, Lucy Murrie, Wash Hamilton, Lyda McClinton, Annie Eugle, W. C. Hamilton, two unidentified, Tom Gaines, Dick Elmore, Iva Hopkins, and unidentified. (Courtesy of Red River County Historical Society Collection.)

In 1902, a crowd is shown waiting to enter Hamilton's Store for an after-Christmas sale. (Courtesy of Red River County Historical Society Collection.)

The Hocker Brothers Hardware is shown in this location at the northeast corner of Cedar and Broadway Streets. The store specialized in buggies, tack, and hardware. The brothers were Clarence, Otis, and Sam Hocker. (Courtesy of Sam Lennox Hocker collection.)

The Clarksville Country Club Lake (North Lake) is shown in this photograph taken c. 1907, which was when it was still under construction. (Courtesy of Red River County Historical Society Collection.)

Members of the Clarksville Country Club are shown in this photograph fishing in the newly constructed lake c. 1912. (Courtesy of Red River County Historical Society Collection.)

The Clarksville Country Club Clubhouse is shown in this 1927 photograph. The clubhouse has been the scene of many dances, parties, wedding receptions, and reunions. (Courtesy of Red River County Historical Society Collection.)

Prior to the construction of bridges, ferries were the only means to cross the Red River. The Bryarly Ferry is shown in this photograph. This ferry was one of the main ferries used to cross to Idabel. There was also a ferry at Albion that remained until the bridge was built in the 1950s. (Courtesy of Lelia Bryarly Bonham Clark collection.)

In the early 1920s, a toll bridge was built to cross Red River at the community of Watson. This bridge is shown in a 1921 photograph. The bridge was washed away in a flood soon after its construction. (Courtesy of Red River County Historical Society Collection.)

The South Lake Clubhouse is shown in this postcard *c.* 1920. (Courtesy of Eugene W. Bowers collection.)

The Clarksville Post Office was built in 1914 and is shown in this postcard *c.* 1920. (Courtesy of Eugene W. Bowers collection.)

The Brewer Hotel is shown in this photograph c. 1930. The hotel served as a lodging place for many years for drummers (salesmen) and travelers. It was torn down in the 1970s. (Courtesy of Red River County Historical Society Collection.)

Shown here is the interior of the Hart Anderson Drug Company on the north side of the Clarksville Square. This photograph was taken in the 1920s before the removal of the soda fountain. (Courtesy of Red River County Historical Society Collection.)

The employees of Hart Anderson Drug Company are shown here in this *c.* 1940 photograph. Those pictured are, from left to right, J. C. Hart (Owner), Charlie Anderson (Owner), Ernest Collins, unidentified, and R. T. Marchbanks. (Courtesy of Red River County Historical Society Collection.)

The Texas and Pacific Railroad came through Red River County in 1876, and the Clarksville depot was built soon thereafter on North Cedar Street at the tracks. This red brick structure served for many years and had many changes until it was torn down in the 1970s. (Courtesy of Red River County Historical Society Collection.)

A crowd waits for the arrival of the train from Texarkana in this 1920s-era photograph. The Paris Grocer Company may be seen in the background on the right and the Clarksville Compress on the left. (Courtesy of Red River County Historical Society Collection.)

In this 1913 photograph, cars wait to greet those coming home on the train at the Clarksville Texas and Pacific Railroad depot. A common pastime was to wait at the depot to watch the comings and goings of those on the train. (Courtesy of Red River County Historical Society Collection.)

The Annona Texas and Pacific Railroad depot, where Ira Bishop was the stationmaster, is shown in this photograph. Annona was known as Walker's Station before the coming of the railroad. (Courtesy of Red River County Historical Society Collection.)

This photograph is of the interior of the First National Bank located on the southeast corner of the square. The photograph was taken in 1902 after the erection of the new building. Those pictured include, from left to right, John Latimer, W. B. Look, A. A. Strange, unidentified, A. D. "Boog" Lennox, Floyd Wren, and E. M. Bowers. (Courtesy of Eugene W. Bowers collection.)

This view is of the interior of the First National Bank after it moved into the former home of the City National Bank on the southwest corner of the Clarksville Square. Those pictured, from left to right, include the following: Tim Aubrey, Bernard Sunkel, Mary Heston Dick, Eugene W. Bowers, Ethel Kirk, and Guy Shackleford. (Courtesy of Eugene W. Bowers collection.)

The Anderson Buick Company was one of Clarksville's earlier automobile dealerships. Alva Anderson is shown in this photograph (with hand on car) with one of Buick's latest models. (Courtesy of Red River County Historical Society Collection.)

J. W. Allen and Brother was formed in 1907 and later became Allen Lumber Company. An entry that they had in the 1914 fair parade is shown in this photograph. (Courtesy of Red River County Historical Society Collection.)

This photograph of the interior of the Red River National Bank, which was taken c. 1925, shows the great precautions that were taken to safeguard the cashiers. Of note is the sign hanging in the teller cage offering a $5,000 reward for dead bank robbers. Those pictured include, from left to right, C. E. Williams, Tom Hutchison, Charles Canterbury, unidentified, and Bertram Dean Wren. (Courtesy of Richard D. "Dick" Wren collection.)

In 1938, the interior of the Red River National Bank had seen some changes with the removal of the teller cages. Additional modifications were made to the lobby and the outside of the building after fire damage occurred when the Hub building burned in 1944. (Courtesy of Red River County Historical Society Collection.)

The McKenzie Meadow, which was southwest of Clarksville, was a popular destination for buggy rides in the 1890s. This meadow provided hay for the animals of McKenzie College. This photograph was taken in 1895. (Courtesy of Red River County Historical Society Collection.)

The harvesting of hay was a busy time and required much labor before the advent of modern mechanical devices. This photograph was taken in 1902 at the Lennox hay meadow, which was south of Clarksville. The Lennox children and their friends may be seen in the wagon. (Courtesy of Red River County Historical Society Collection.)

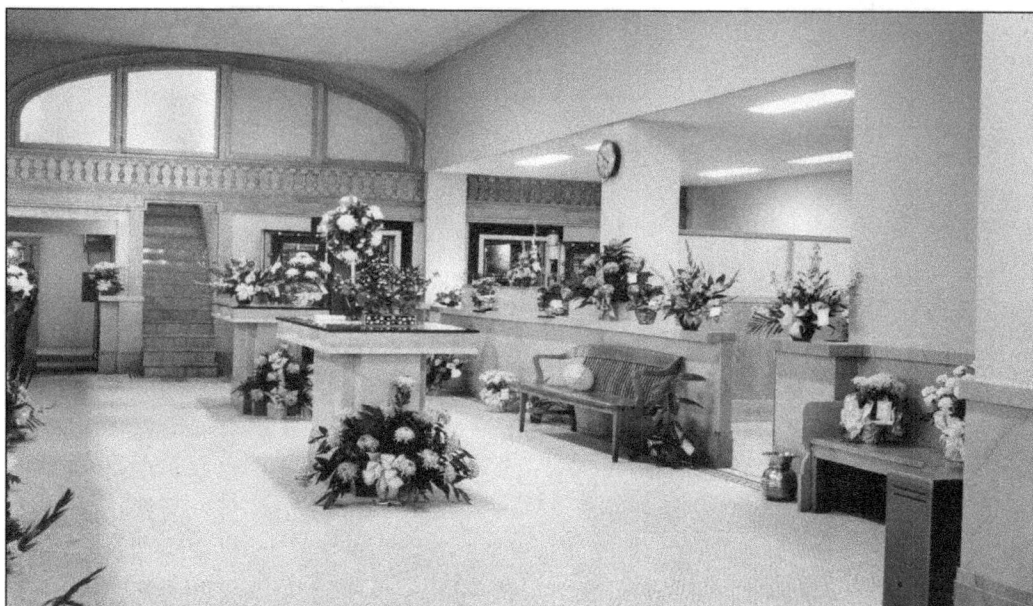

A fire in 1955 did extensive smoke and water damage to the lobby and offices of the First National Bank. This photograph shows the newly remodeled lobby on the reopening day. (Courtesy of Red River County Historical Society Collection.)

The Red River Lumber Company was located west of Bagwell and was one of the area's largest sawmills. Ed Jones owned it. This aerial view of the lumberyard was taken in 1956. (Courtesy of Jan Jones Smith collection.)

The Dairy Mart was a favorite gathering place of Clarksville High School students in the 1950s and 1960s. It was located on the northeast corner of Main and Donoho Streets. The students in this 1957 photograph are, from left to right, Max Hardee, Patsy Petty, Bill Petty, Linda McDonough, Joe Alice Russell, and James Paul Harvey. (Courtesy of Red River County Historical Society Collection.)

The Top Drive-In was located on East Main Street in Clarksville. It was also a favorite gathering place for students and adults alike. Jake Holster founded the business. (Courtesy of Red River County Historical Society Collection.)

The Red River Drive-In Movie was located southwest of Clarksville on the new Bogata Road and served outdoor moviegoers for 20 years. (Courtesy of Anne Russell Evetts collection.)

J. W. Nichols Ladies Wear was founded on the south side of the Clarksville Square in 1938 by Nick and Evelyn Nichols and was later owned by their son John and his wife, Nancy. The store burned in 1950 and was replaced by this building shown. (Courtesy of John M. Nichols collection.)

Eight

CLARKSVILLE SCHOOLS

The Clarksville Grammar School was built in 1887 and torn down in 1948. It was located on College Avenue at Delaware Street. Graded public schools were established in Clarksville in 1880 in a wooden school building, which was replaced by this building. (Courtesy of Red River County Historical Society Collection.)

McKenzie College, three miles southwest of Clarksville, was organized by John W. P. McKenzie in 1841 in a log cabin. By 1854, it had 300 students and 9 faculty members. The college had an administration building and three dormitories, two for boys and one for girls. Its equipment was considered first class, and the library probably had between 2,000 and 3,000 volumes. The students are shown in this photograph in front of one of the dormitories in this very early photograph dating to the early 1860s. (Courtesy of Red River County Historical Society Collection.)

McKenzie College—for several years the largest college in Texas—was always a Methodist institution, although it was actually controlled by the Methodist Conference for one year only. It trained almost all of the Texas Methodist ministers of the period. McKenzie deeded the school to the church in 1855 but on conditions that the conference could not fulfill. Again in 1860, he made a conditional deed of the property to the conference. By the summer of 1861, most of the student body had gone into the Confederate Army, and the church returned the property to McKenzie. The school adapted itself to the times by offering military drill to students. In 1863, enrollment dropped to 33, and the average enrollment from 1864 to 1867 was 74 students. McKenzie and his son-in-law, Smith Ragsdale, no longer able to keep the school financially independent, closed it on June 25, 1868. The administration building is shown in this 1860-era photograph. (Courtesy of Red River County Historical Society Collection.)

Clarksville High School was built in 1916 and served students until burning in 1987. (Courtesy of Red River County Historical Society Collection.)

The Clarksville High School Gymnasium is shown in the photograph. The building faced south on Washington Avenue and was built in the early 1930s. In addition to sporting events, many dances, Halloween carnivals, and other entertainments were held in this building. (Courtesy of Red River County Historical Society Collection.)

Clarksville Elementary School was built in 1948 on Washington Avenue to replace the old Grammar School. This building continues to serve the academic needs of Clarksville schoolchildren today. (Courtesy of Red River County Historical Society Collection.)

St. Joseph Academy was established in 1873. Classes were held in this building and at an annex building until the school was disbanded and absorbed into the Clarksville Public Schools in 1934. (Courtesy of St. Joseph Catholic Church Collection.)

Shown here is the 1925 Clarksville High School Football Team. Those in the photograph are, from left to right, (first row) Gladney Vick, Moody Hale, Wayne West, Peter Barnett (captain), Hubert Goodman, William Hogan, and Mack Grant; (second row) Clifton Cook, Durn Morris, Thomas Grant, Harold Connell, Gaines Sivley, and Thomas McConnell; (third row) Paul Thompson (manager) and Sam Humphrey (coach). (Courtesy of Red River County Historical Society Collection.)

The Clarksville High School 1933 District Champion Football Team is pictured here on the front steps of the high school. From left to right, those pictured include (first row) J. K. Crain, Dwight Heald, Harold Wallace, Billy Sunkel, Frank Venoy, Hugh Lowe, Willard McCoy, Ted Bolton, John David Gardner, and Phil Brooks; (second row) Foster Conlan, Carl Bean, M. P. (June) Terry, Weldon McCain, John Cozart, Scott Griffin, Charles McMahan, Donald Fryar, and Sam Gullion; (third row) Floyd Green, Teddy Stroupe, Tom Wall, L. B. Caviness, Billy Pinson, George Skidmore, Norfleet Thompson, and Howard Stanley; (fourth row) Ned O'Neill, coach Ed Bloodworth, Ed Proctor, and Jimmy Adams. (Courtesy of Red River County Historical Society Collection.)

Pictured here is the first girl's basketball team from Clarksville High School. Pictured are, from left to right, Elva Brindley, Maude Grant, Lucile Lassiter, Allie Maude Gaines Wren, Elizabeth Banks Duncan, and Allie Grant Bowers. (Courtesy of Eugene W. Bowers collection.)

Clarksville Grammar School's second grade class is shown in this 1907 photograph. Those pictured are, from left to right, (first row) Bessie Banks, Neva Anderson, Folsom Carter, Esther Corley, Mildred Allen, Elizabeth Weaver, and Nita Wheat; (second row) Collin Teel, Emmett Carter, John A. Bagby, Lucian Moore, Arthur Maxfield, Jennie Bettes, Nannie Baker, and Mable Kerr; (third row) Robert McMaster, Jennie Templeton, Julian Corley, Bagby Lennox, Trammel Sanders, and Willard Moore. (Courtesy of Red River County Historical Society Collection.)

Pictured here is the fourth grade class of the Clarksville Grammar School in 1907. Those pictured are, from left to right, (first row) Gene White, Rob Bloom, Harvey Murphy, Bobby Roliter, Tim Aubrey, and Leonard Cole; (second row) Kitty Latimer, Fay Edwards, Louise Hopkins, Gladys Mehaffey, Kate Gaines, Emma Mae McClinton, Dorothy Taylor, and Midget Cheatham; (third row) Abbie Whiteman, Myrtle Anderson, Annie Strou, Minnie Stinsendopher, Helen Latimer, Mary Smiley, Margaret Watson, Rebecca Cornelius, Gyla Wheat, and Mattie Hure; (fourth row) Ben Marable, Henry Dickson, Ed West, Robert Reed, David Bruton, Louis Hall, David Latimer, David Lennox, Alvin Baker, and John Duncan. (Courtesy of Red River County Historical Society Collection.)

Pictured here is the sixth grade class of Clarksville Grammar School in 1907. Those pictured are, from left to right, (first row) Verna Brewer, Rannie Lennox, Lucile Johnson, Pansy Brown, Raymond Norris, Stewart Stanley, Ethel Poke, Mary Edwards, Henry Allen, Richard Lee Tayloe, Galen Sturgis, Johnnie Burris, and John Porter Aubrey; (second row) Louie Norris, Allie Grant, Ruth Barry, Allie Maud Gaines, Love Teel, Essie Haley, Ira Doak, Rosa Mai Hutchison, Lizzie Mae Banks, and Frellie White; (third row) Henry Whiteman, Plummer Bland, Alex Stephens, Lewis Mehaffey, Robert Raines, Roy Dinwiddie, Gordon Bruton, Ballard Dinwiddie, Gattis Corley, John White, and Erwin Barry. (Courtesy of Red River County Historical Society Collection.)

The sixth grade class of Clarksville Grammar School is shown in this 1918 photograph. Those pictured are, from left to right, (first row) Clifton Cook, Melvin Marx, unidentified, J. T. Arnold, Mack Grant, Red ?, Claude Earl Bruton, and Clark Anderson; (second row) unidentified, Roberta Benningfield, Avanell Wagoner, Nellie Gibbs, Emily Talley, Patsy McKenzie, Martha Lou Robbins, and Rowena Stiles; (third row) Mary Lee Irwin, Frances Cook, Susie Marable, Addie Soward, Naomi Giddens, Lucy Chambers, Martha Lennox, and two unidentified people; (fourth row) Gaines Sivley, unidentified; Elizabeth Tyre, Allie Mae Brewer, unidentified, and Madge Fryar; (fifth row) unidentified, Harold Connell, Paul Steinline, Arthur Athas, unidentified, Pappy Carson, Thomas McConnell, Harry Westmoreland, David Jackson, Red Isbell, Payne Ward, Willie Smith, and Ernest Sutton Collins. (Courtesy of Red River County Historical Society Collection.)

Nine

CITIZENS

Isabella Haddon Hopkins Hanks Clark Gordon was born in 1805 in Kentucky and came to Texas in 1827. After her first husband, John Hanks, died, she married James Clark in 1829, and they lived at Jonesboro on the Red River. It was in their home that Sam Houston spent his first night in Texas. The Clarks moved to the black land prairie in 1833 and founded Clarksville. After Clark's death in 1838, Isabella married Dr. George Gordon. She was a great philanthropist, donating lots for businesses and churches so that the town would grow. She died in 1895. (Courtesy of Clark family collection.)

Col. Charles DeMorse is shown here in this early photograph at his printing press in *The Standard* offices on North Locust Street. DeMorse served as editor and publisher of this paper, which was the second-oldest newspaper in Texas. He also served as colonel in the 29th Texas Cavalry in the War Between the States. (Courtesy of Mary H. Hausler collection.)

Benjamin Epperson was a lawyer, politician, and state legislator. He was born in Amite County, Mississippi, in 1826. He attended Princeton University but did not graduate. He moved to Texas sometime before 1847 and settled in Clarksville, which was where he studied law and was admitted to the bar. Though he was young, he was immediately accepted as a community leader. After brief service as a county commissioner, he was elected to the Second Texas Legislature in 1847. By 1860, he was one of the wealthiest men in the state. In 1871, he moved to Jefferson, where the next year he built the House of the Seasons. This was an unusual structure that was built in the style of an Italian villa. The seasons were represented by the four colors of glass in its cupola. Epperson died in 1878. (Courtesy of Eugene W. Bowers collection.)

The Clarksville Brass Band is shown in this 1892 photograph. From left to right, the members of the band are (first row) Al Corley, Mr. McAlester, and George Hilliard; (second row) Mr. Reed, A. P. Dick Jr., E. P. Gaines, Pres Corley, Frank Hooks, and Frank Miesch. (Courtesy of Eugene W. Bowers collection.)

The Clarksville Pig Club is shown in this 1913 photograph in front of the Red River National Bank. Those pictured are, from left to right, Will McMaster (county agent, barely visible), Jack Duncan, Morgan Graves (president of Red River National Bank), Frank Wright, Jack Crader, Jim Crader, two unidentified, Red Davis, Clarence Humphrey, Paul Hale, John Russell Anderson, Collier Miesch, John Peck, Wilson Bloodworth, Henry Smith, Harold Hooks, George Sunkel, and unidentified. (Courtesy of Red River County Historical Society Collection.)

In the summer of 1893, a group of roughly 120 Red River County veterans joined in forming a veteran's organization called the John C. Burk's Camp of United Confederate Veterans. These men held a reunion every summer for almost 40 years. Two to three days were set aside for this event, and thousands of people converged on Clarksville. The Confederate Reunion Pavilion is shown in this photograph. The reunion grounds were located just south of the present Langford Lake. (Courtesy of Red River County Historical Society Collection.)

This group of Confederate veterans is pictured at one of the last reunions. Programs were given throughout the reunion by the Clarksville band and the talented musicians of the time. Choruses from the school also sang, and there were numerous speakers. As time passed, carnivals became very popular at the reunion. (Courtesy of Red River County Historical Society Collection.)

This photograph was taken at the Confederate Reunion in 1921. Many of those attending brought camping equipment and remained on the event's grounds. Those who came each day brought lunches packed in washtubs or trunks and spread them under the beautiful trees of the reunion grounds, as this photograph depicts. (Courtesy of Red River County Historical Society Collection.)

The Donoho carriage is shown at the Confederate Reunion in this photograph. Those pictured are, from left to right, Frank Marable, Frank Latimer, Durwood Cooper, Mary Donoho, Nellie Donoho, Blanche Trilling, Dr. Barton, Frank Reed, and Will Hamilton. (Courtesy of Red River County Historical Society Collection.)

Pictured is the staging of a wedding with local businessmen playing the roles of bride, groom, and wedding party. This was a fundraiser that was held at the Clarksville Country Club in the early 1930s. Those pictured are, from left to right, Ramie Price, Harold Summers, Richard Lee Tayloe, Frank Marable, Ballard Dinwiddie, Carlin O'Neill, Leighton Reed, Morgan Graves, Ritchie McCulloch, Jonathan Latimer, unidentified, Erwin Barry, unidentified, Bagby Lennox, unidentified, Elmore McClinton, and Pat Graves. (Courtesy of Red River County Historical Society Collection.)

Shown here are children attending Fay Nichols' birthday party at her home on East Broadway Street in 1909. Those pictured are, from left to right, (first row) Kitty Cook, Kathryn Bettes, Elma Cornelius, Bit Webb, Margaret Marable, and Edith Butcher; (second row) L. T. Russell, Nick Athas, Louis Tayloe, Son Owens, William Tayloe, Graves Dickson, Dot Latimer, and Inez Latimer; (third row) Olga Athas, Fay Nichols, Maurien Grant, Mary Sudie Moore, Kelsey Dick, Rosine Dickson, Lelia Grigsby, Margaret Cooper, and Hallie Payne Webb. (Courtesy of Red River County Historical Society Collection.)

After a name suggested by Ella Watson, the Entre Nous Dinner Club was formed in the 1930s. The members had dinner once a month at a participant's home. Those seated are, from left to right, (first row) Byron Black, Frances Marx, and Jerold Marx; (second row) Melvin Marx Jr., Grant Walker, F. F. "Son" Marable, Don Black, June Brewer, and unidentified; (side row) Winnie Mattie Walker, Loyce Brewer, Ann Black, and Homer Pope; (third row) Randolph Osburn, LaVerne Osburn, three unidentified people, Margaret Pope, and Audrey Black. The couple on the far left is unidentified. (Courtesy of Red River County Historical Society, gift of Audrey Graves Black.)

The Clarksville Business and Professional Women's Club held their 1946 Christmas Party at the home of Essie Walker. Among those pictured are Noda Grant, Fannie Look, Essie Walker, Vera Adams, Grace Lawrence, Anna Patterson, Cora Wright, Mary Hunter Jackson, Elizabeth Williams, Bess Hughston, Willie Mae Witmer, Minnie Witmer, Lillian Fisher, Louise Kelty, Helen Felker, Billie Bartley, Agnes Scaff, Belle Howland, Thelma Greer, Ruby Goodman, Beulah Smith, Winnie Kelty, Grace Mikel, Mary Reed, Bernice Seay, Merle Ferguson, Virginia Hudson, Clyde McDonald, Betty Pretty, Opal Abercrombie, Rebecca Monts, and Addie Aubrey. (Courtesy of Red River County Historical Society Collection.)

A costume party was held at the Clarksville Country Club in 1948. Among those pictured are ? McCluer, Audrey Graves Black, Swann Sivley Sims, David Lennox, Winnie Mattie Walker, Dorothy Bonham, Dorothea Pewitt, Ernest Pewitt, Loyce Brewer (partially hidden), Nancy Wright Hogue, Reeves "Bully" Hogue, Mot Wright, Mary Catherine Puckett, Furman Wolf, Donald Chain Black Sr., Barbara Wolf, Ann Ezell Black, and Frances Marx. (Courtesy of Red River County Historical Society Collection.)

Those at the costume party are, from left to right, Audrey Graves Black (partially hidden), Frances Marx, Mary Bonham, Ed Bonham, ? Haly, unidentified, ? Haly, Ida Friedman, Charley Freedman, three unidentified, Fay Nichols Fowler, Frank Fowler, three unidentified, Helen Marable, F. F. "Son" Marable Jr., Jimmy Latimer, Dorothea Pewitt, Ernest Pewitt, Grace Latimer, Bagby Lennox, and unidentified. (Courtesy of Red River County Historical Society Collection.)

Among those pictured are Byron B. Black, Audrey Graves Black, ? McCluer, Sally Crosthwaite, George Crosthwaite, Mary Graves West, Peyton West, Meda Reed, Billie Miesch, Eugena Milan Hughston, Tommie Ross Hughston, Grace Latimer, Jimmy Latimer, LaVerne Osburn, Lela May Wooley Beadle, and Pat C. Beadle. (Courtesy of Red River County Historical Society Collection.)

From left to right, the winners of the best costumes were Bagby Lennox, Loyce Brewer, Ed Bonham, Esther Maude Harvey, Clifton Kay, and Evelyn Nichols. (Courtesy of Red River County Historical Society Collection.)

Gussie Simpson hosted a dinner party at her home honoring her son Alex and his new bride, Mary, in 1949. Those pictured are, from left to right, (front table) Dixie Peek Goodman, Dean Burtner, James Ellis Goodman, and Nancy Womack Burtner; (back table) Martene Holland Watson, Mary Edrington Edwards, Richard D. "Dick" Wren, Ben Edwards and Gavin Watson Jr.; (right table) Alex Simpson, Joan Sims Vaughan, Dr. Nowlin Watson, and Mary Crawford Simpson. (Courtesy of Richard D. "Dick" Wren collection.)

The officers and employees of the Red River National Bank are shown in this photograph at the opening of the new bank in 1965. Those pictured are, from left to right, (first row) Byron B. Black Sr., T. G. Miller, Bill Bettes, Connie Kay Lindeman, Betty Mauldin Sargent, Louise Eudy, Tiny Lynch, Charles Canterbury, Alex Simpson, and A. D. Simpson; (second row) Jessie Calhoun, Betty Westfall, Kelsey Dick, and Giles McCarver. (Courtesy of Red River County Historical Society Collection.)

Visit us at
arcadiapublishing.com

www.ingramcontent.com/pod-product-compliance
Lightning Source LLC
Chambersburg PA
CBHW080612110426
42813CB00006B/1487